PRAISE FOR
GROWING FRIENDSHIPS

Funny, practical, and not at all preachy—*Growing Friendships* offers spot-on, research-based friendship advice for girls AND boys. Highly recommended! This must-read book is the Google Maps to friendship that every kid needs.

Michele Borba, author of *Unselfie*

Growing Friendships is the secret playbook you'll wish you'd had when you were growing up. It's packed with clever strategies that help kids handle the awkward, upsetting, and confusing social situations that happen to everyone. The fun cartoons make the advice light-hearted and easy to swallow.

Diane Debrovner, deputy editor of *Parents* magazine

In our fast-paced and disruptive world, we're losing sight of the kitchen-table wisdom that children used to take refuge in. This book puts kids and their parents back in touch with basic, tried and true, social skills, and the ways in which those skills can be used.

Retailing Insight

Kennedy-Moore and McLaughlin highlight five skills—reaching out, stepping back, blending in, speaking up, and letting go—to help readers make and maintain friendships. Mingus's cartoon spot illustrations and comics sequences add humor and help illustrate various points [while] multiple-choice quizzes and reader-directed questions invite children to apply these ideas to their own developing relationships.

Publishers Weekly

Practical examples, real-life solutions, and playful humor make *Growing Friendships* a great resource. This insightful guide can help kids become competent problem solvers, cope with common social challenges, develop empathy, and build strong friendships.

Tina Payne Bryson, PhD, coauthor of bestsellers
The Whole-Brain Child and *No-Drama Discipline*

This book is so important! All children face friendship challenges at some point and *Growing Friendships* offers kids real help—and enough giggles to make the messages fun and memorable.

Amy McCready, author of
If I Have to Tell You One More Time and *The "Me, Me, Me" Epidemic*

The complexities of friendships in the school-aged years can be the most perplexing for students, parents, and educators alike. *Growing Friendships* gives research-based, concrete, and effective solutions for navigating these relationships. A tool every school should have!

Kelly Bos, MSW, RSW, psychotherapist, parent, and former school counselor

Some kids intuitively know how to make and manage friendships. Most don't. *Growing Friendships* is a kid-friendly guide that uses simple language, engaging illustrations, and humor to help girls AND boys master the mysteries of social interaction.

Jennifer L.W. Fink, founder of BuildingBoys.net

The author team of Kennedy-Moore and McLaughlin offers sound advice from the perspectives of psychologist, parent, blogger, and therapist. This is an authoritative and appealing resource for children working on fitting in and finding a tribe.

Erin Anderson, *Booklist*

This empowering and entertaining guide for kids shows ways to maneuver the often tricky, confusing, and challenging journey to build and maintain positive friendships. Not only do children learn strategies to make new friends, handle stressful situations, say "no" to a pushy peer, and be a great team member, *Growing Friendships* makes the process fun and meaningful for the entire family.

Marilyn Price-Mitchell, PhD, developmental psychologist and founder of Roots of Action

Eileen Kennedy-Moore brings a wealth of experience, knowledge, and sensitivity to this issue. Her book *Growing Friendships* . . . will be an invaluable tool for parents and professionals as they try to prevent their child from hearing the most dreaded words in childhood: *"Sorry, you can't sit there. That seat's taken."*

Richard D. Lavoie, author of *It's So Much Work to be Your Friend*

Finally! A gap in the literature of friendship is filled. *Growing Friendships* is profound and subtle, clear and humorous. Anyone, of any age, who reads it will benefit.

Wendy Mogel, PhD, author of *The Blessing of a Skinned Knee*

This spot-on guide navigates the slippery slope of inevitable difficulties with kid humor and compassion to demonstrate not only how to mend friendships or let them go, but also how to be a good friend. If you have school-age children they—and you—need this book.

Susan Newman, PhD, social psychologist and author of
Little Things Long Remembered and *The Case for the Only Child*

A decent guide for younger middle grade collections, even adults could learn something from this book.

School Library Journal

For any child struggling with friendships, this book will be a source of comfort, guidance, and fun, with its wonderful illustrations and child-centered dialogue. Counselors, psychologists, and parents, this is a book to read with the children you care about.

Maurice J. Elias, PhD, Rutgers University, coauthor of
The Joys and Oys of Parenting and *Emotionally Intelligent Parenting*

A KIDS' GUIDE TO
Making and Keeping Friends

GROWING FRIENDSHIPS

Dr. Eileen Kennedy-Moore
& Christine McLaughlin

ALADDIN
New York London Toronto Sydney New Delhi

BEYOND WORDS
Portland, Oregon

ALADDIN
An imprint of Simon & Schuster
Children's Publishing Division
1230 Avenue of the Americas
New York, NY 10020

BEYOND WORDS
1750 S.W. Skyline Blvd., Suite 20
Portland, Oregon 97221-2543
503-531-8700 / 503-531-8773 fax
www.beyondword.com

This Beyond Words/Aladdin edition July 2017
Text copyright © 2017 by Eileen Kennedy-Moore and Christine McLaughlin
Cover and interior illustrations copyright © 2017 by Beyond Words/Simon & Schuster, Inc.
Cover copyright © 2023 by Beyond Words/Simon & Schuster, Inc.

The vignettes in this book are based on dialogues with children the authors have known. The characters are composites and so no real names have been used. The dialogues represent typical behavior and problems, and they do not refer to specific people or real events. This book is for educational purposes only. It does not constitute and should not substitute for individual professional advice, psychotherapy, or the provision of psychological services.

ALADDIN and related logo are registered trademarks of Simon & Schuster, Inc.
BEYOND WORDS PUBLISHING and related logo are registered trademarks of Beyond Words Publishing. Beyond Words is an imprint of Simon & Schuster, Inc.

For information about special discounts for bulk purchases, please contact Simon & Schuster Special Sales at 1-866-506-1949 or business@simonandschuster.com.

The Simon & Schuster Speakers Bureau can bring authors to your live event. For more information or to book an event contact the Simon & Schuster Speakers Bureau at 1-866-248-3049 or visit our website at www.simonspeakers.com.

Managing Editor: Lindsay S. Easterbrooks-Brown
Editor: Nicole Geiger
Copyediting: Jade Chan, Emmalisa Sparrow Wood
Proofreader: Michelle Blair
Illustrator: Cathi Mingus
Interior and cover design: Sara E. Blum
The text of this book was set in Adobe Garamond Pro.

Manufactured in the United States of America 0623 BVG

10

Library of Congress Cataloging-in-Publication Data

Names: Kennedy-Moore, Eileen, author. | McLaughlin, Christine, author.
Title: Growing friendships : a kids' guide to making and keeping friends /
  Eileen Kennedy-Moore and Christine McLaughlin.
Description: New York : Aladdin ; Hillsboro, Oregon : Beyond Words, 2017.
Identifiers: LCCN 2016019719 | ISBN 9781582705880 (paperback) |
  ISBN 9781582705897 (hardcover) | ISBN 9781481466462 (eBook)
Subjects: LCSH: Friendship in children—Juvenile literature. | Interpersonal
  relations in children—Juvenile literature. | Social skills in
  children—Juvenile literature.
Classification: LCC BF723.F68 K456 2017 | DDC 155.4/1925—dc23
LC record available at https://lccn.loc.gov/2016019719

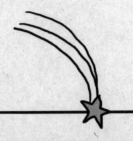

FOR OUR CHILDREN AND OUR NIECES AND NEPHEWS—
BECAUSE COUSIN-FRIENDS ARE EXTRA SPECIAL!

CONTENTS

NOTE TO GROWN-UPS

Research tells us that friendship is complicated for kids. Among first graders, one-half of best-friendships don't last the whole school year. Even for late-elementary and middle-school kids, one-quarter of their best-friendships don't make it from September to June. That's a lot of breakups.

Almost every child struggles socially at some time, in some way. Having an argument with a friend, getting teased, or even trying to find a buddy in a new classroom . . . although these are typical problems, they can be very painful for both girls and boys.

Friendship skills are never about just doing one thing. Children need to be able to be flexible and adjust their behavior to fit the situation. They need to be able to **Reach Out** to make friends, but they also need to know when they're doing something off-putting so they can **Step Back** to respect a friend's feelings. It's great when kids can **Blend In** to enjoy the camaraderie of a group, but they also need to be able to **Speak Up** and say, "No, this isn't right for me," or "This is what I want." Finally, because no one is perfect, kids need to be able to **Let Go** to move past difficulties and open their hearts to forgiveness.

Growing Friendships gives kids the answers they need to make and keep friends. Some kids will prefer reading this book on their own, but reading it with your child can spark discussion that connects the ideas to your child's real life experience, and help you be an effective social coach for them. You can start at the beginning or jump to the sections that are most relevant for your child at that moment. Don't try to cover everything in one sitting. There's a lot of information here! *Growing Friendships* is a guide you and your child can return to again and again whenever need arises.

Eileen Kennedy-Moore, PhD, and Christine McLaughlin

PART I
Reaching Out to Make Friends

Have you ever wished you had more friends? Most kids do at some point. Maybe your friends are in a different class this year. Or maybe your best friend moved away. Maybe you're starting at a new school. Maybe you're just not getting along with your old friends the way you used to. This part of *Growing Friendships* is all about **Reaching Out** to make new friends. Whatever your reason is for wanting more friends, the next three chapters will give you lots of ideas about how to make them.

1
Take First Steps

BRANDON'S CHALLENGE: FEELING ALONE

Brandon wishes he had someone to play with at recess, but he doesn't know how to connect with others. His body language—looking away, standing apart, even tuning everyone out by reading his book—tells them, "I don't like you, and I don't want to hang out with you!" That's not what he's feeling, but that's the message he's sending.

What can Brandon do to Reach Out to other kids and show them he's interested in being friends?

SAYING HELLO

Have you ever noticed what happens when you arrive at school? Kids say, "Hi!" And they don't just announce "Hi!" to the air. They greet specific people. They look them in the eye, they smile, and they often say the other person's name. Try this experiment: The next day you go to school, count how many greetings you hear. You may be surprised by how often kids greet each other.

Greeting people tells them you're happy to see them. It's also important to smile and say hi back when someone greets you. If you look away and say nothing or just mumble something, the other person might think you don't want to be friends.

You may want to practice friendly greetings. They won't instantly get you friends, but they open the door to friendship. The more you practice greetings, the more comfortable you'll feel doing them.

Start by greeting family members. Then think of kids at school you can greet. Use your face and your body language to show that you're happy to see them. Use their names to make the greeting personal. And be ready to respond in a friendly way when someone greets you.

WHY FRIENDLY GREETINGS MATTER

Sometimes kids don't want to greet others because they worry that they won't get a response. They're afraid of feeling foolish or getting rejected and being embarrassed. But you'll stand out more if you *don't* greet people.

You don't have to be best friends with people to greet them. You just have to know them a little bit and think they're nice. A friendly greeting takes only a few seconds but it goes a long way toward setting a positive tone and showing other kids that you're interested in being friends.

What happens after "Hi!"? Keep doing friendly things to show that you like them. You can do these right after the greeting or later. Here are some ideas you can try:

1. Ask interested questions.
Asking questions shows someone you want to know more about them. The best questions to ask begin with *what* or *how* because they tend to get longer answers that can lead to a conversation. One or two questions is usually enough at one time. More than that gets annoying. You don't want to turn the conversation into an interview!

Avoid asking *why* questions because they can sound mean. It can seem like you're asking, "Why did you do such a dumb thing?!" even when you're not.

2. Give an honest compliment. It feels good to get a compliment, and we tend to like people who notice and appreciate our good qualities. Keep your eyes open for ways that you can compliment other kids. Compliments

don't have to be long or complicated, but they must be honest. If someone gives you a compliment, be sure to smile and say, "Thanks!"

3. Do a small act of kindness.

Being kind is a great way to start a friendship. An act of *small kindness* tells kids that you like them and it makes you feel good. Be careful not to give away money or favorite things of yours. If the act of kindness is too big, the other kids might feel pressured, and you might feel bad if they don't return the favor.

9

2
Find Common Ground

**RAVEN'S CHALLENGE:
TRYING TO IMPRESS**

CONNECTING, NOT IMPRESSING

Raven wants to be friends with the other kids, but she's going about it in the wrong way. She's focusing on impressing them when she should be thinking about connecting with them.

Some kids believe in the **Magnet Myth of Friendship.** They think that all they have to do is be so amazing and wonderful that they'll attract friends the way a magnet attracts metal. That's not how friendship works.

The Magnet Myth of Friendship is just that—a myth. It isn't true. Friendship is about enjoying each other's company, not proving how great you are. Trying to impress people will not help you make friends, and could even make them dislike you.

BUILD FRIENDSHIPS BASED ON WHAT YOU BOTH LIKE

Raven wants people to admire her, but the other kids aren't interested in being her audience and applauding her. She is probably thinking, "Please like me!" but her bragging tells them, "I think I'm better than you!" That's not a good way to make friends.

Why not? Because friendship is built on **Common Ground,** which are the things you both like. Here's a picture of a friendship between two boys, Ryan and Drew:

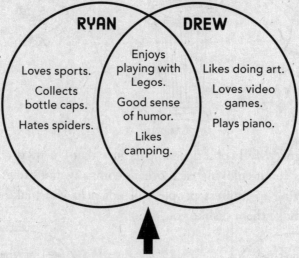

Where friendship begins.

The overlap in the center is their Common Ground. It shows things that both boys enjoy that they can have a good time doing together. This is where friendship grows. On the other hand, the interests that belong to only one of the boys, like sports for Ryan and art for Drew, are not directly part of the friendship and won't bring them together. After they are already friends, they may enjoy and appreciate each other's differences, but it's the overlap that matters for starting and continuing a friendship. Kids who don't have much in common probably won't become friends.

WHAT YOU BOTH LIKE

Friends don't have to be exactly alike. No two people ever are. But when you're building a friendship, you need to figure out what you and the other kid have in common. You don't have to hide differences, but you do need to look for similarities. In a new relationship, pointing out how you're different separates you, but figuring out how you're the same can bring you together.

If you talk to someone about something outside your overlap—something that only one of you is interested in—it doesn't build your friendship. For instance, if you tell someone who isn't interested in video games lots of details about how well you did playing your favorite video game, you might bore that person. Or it might even seem like you're bragging, just like Raven did at the start of this chapter. Telling people that you are better than them will not make them like you.

Kids usually become friends by doing things together. Having fun together builds real connections. What do you like doing? Who else do you know who likes doing that? You could become friends with that person!

If you're not sure whether someone likes the same activities you do, there's an easy way to find out: ask! Remember those interested questions we talked about in the last chapter (page 7)? Try asking some of them!

FIGURE IT OUT

Here's a list of some things kids have in common. Which do you think would help build a friendship and why?

a. Sharon and Tricia both have Ls in their last name.

b. Mario and Nathan are both Cubs fans.

c. Stephanie and Melissa both enjoy doing crafts.

d. Darius and Mikhail are both left-handed.

e. Aparna and Meaghan are on the same soccer team.

f. George and Hiram both get in trouble a lot at school.

g. Lindsey and Carmen both have messy bedrooms.

h. Ben and Alex both collect baseball cards.

Answers: *b, c, e, h*. Remember that people become friends by doing fun things together. Sentence *f* describes something the boys both do, but it's not a good base for a healthy friendship.

3
Take It Slow

**ANGELA'S CHALLENGE:
HOLDING ON TOO TIGHT**

Angela is being an **Octopus Friend.** She is grabbing her friend Vanessa and squeezing her so tightly that she can hardly move. This probably doesn't feel good to Vanessa. No one likes to feel trapped. If Angela keeps trying to control Vanessa, Vanessa is going to want to escape. Angela is afraid of losing Vanessa as a friend, but the way she's acting could end up pushing Vanessa away.

18

It's important to Reach Out to make friends, but you don't want to be an Octopus Friend like Angela. Let your friends have other friends. Let some time pass—maybe two or three weeks—between invitations. You want your friends to miss you a little bit. You also want to give them a chance to seek out your company or invite you over.

Keep in mind that you don't have to have just one friend. Having more than one friend gives you more options. If one friend is absent or if you're having an argument with a friend, you'll still have other kids to play with.

You can also have different kinds of friends.

Having different kinds of friends makes your life more interesting. Some friends are closer or more special than others, but all friends are people you can have fun with.

You can also try to become closer with the friends of your friends. If you try to force a friend to choose between you and another kid, you will probably lose that friend. No one likes to feel pulled in two different directions, like the rope in a game of tug-of-war.

Friendship Tug-of-War

MORE FRIENDS, MORE FUN

Instead of trying to keep your friend all to yourself, try to be open to other people your friend likes. If you can all be friends, then your friend doesn't have to choose only one of you. Reaching Out to the other friend is a kind thing to do and it expands your circle of friendship.

Sometimes groups of three can have trouble getting along because one person always feels left out. If that's happening to you, you may want to add a fourth person to your friend group. Just start inviting that person along when the three of you are doing something fun. Four buddies playing together is practically a party!

Getting together as a group—at school, at after-school activities, or at home—is one way to keep your close friend and expand your friendship circle. Sometimes, you may also want to get together with different people. Maybe there's someone you'd like to get to know better, or maybe you'd like to reconnect with an old friend you haven't seen much lately.

A one-on-one play date is one of the best things you can do to deepen a new or existing friendship. Inviting someone over is a very nice compliment because it says, "I like you, and I'd like to spend more time with you." It also gives you a chance to focus on just each other. If you've been arguing with a friend, having a fun one-on-one play date (without arguing!) can help you remember what you enjoy about each other.

INVITE FRIENDS WISELY

Angela, the girl in the cartoon at the start of this chapter, had the right idea when she wanted to invite her friend over; she was just trying to do *too much* of a good thing by overwhelming her friend with too many invitations. It's a good idea to spread out your play date invitations to different people and to let some time pass before you invite the same person again.

Try to invite someone who likes to do the same things you like to do. You don't have to be close friends with someone to invite them over.

If you've had fun together a time or two at school or during an after-school activity, then you know each other well enough to get together outside school and take your friendship to a deeper level.

Once you decide who you want to invite, the next step is to talk to your grown-ups about when would be some good times to have your friend over. Come up with two dates or times so you can work around your friend's plans if needed.

If you're in fourth grade or older, it's a good idea for you to take the lead in setting up the play date, rather than having a grown-up do it. You'll need to get permission first, but you should be the one to invite your friend. You can do this in person, by phone, email, or text, depending on what's comfortable for you and what you're allowed to do. A phone call is often best because you'll know your friend received the invitation, and it makes it easy to adjust and agree on plans. When you invite your friend, say that you were wondering if they could come over and suggest a time. If your friend is busy, suggest the second time. If your friend still can't do it, say, "Well, maybe another time," and Let It Go (We'll go more into this topic in Part V). You don't want to be too pushy. You can try making a play date with that friend in a couple of weeks.

If the first person you invite can't come over, think of someone else you can invite over.

PLAY DATE TIPS

Once you've scheduled a play date, here are some guidelines to make sure it goes well:

Prepare the scene. If there are toys you'll have trouble sharing, put them away before your friend arrives. Think of activities your friend might enjoy doing with you at your home. Ask your grown-ups if they'll prepare a nice snack for you and your friend.

Welcome your friend. When your friend arrives, greet them with a smile and offer two suggestions of things to do. Offering your friend two choices avoids an awkward moment where you both don't know what to do. ("What do you want to do?" "I don't know. What do you want to do?")

Treat your friend well. As the host, it's your job to make sure your friend has a good time. Stay with your friend, rather than going off by yourself or

playing with someone else. Make sure your friend is involved and playing with you, rather than just watching you do something. Try to do what the friend wants to do and avoid arguing or being bossy. If your friend seems bored or frustrated, suggest another activity or have a snack.

End on a happy note. When it's time to go, accept the end of the play date calmly. Don't make a fuss or hide or try to drag things out because that will annoy the adults and might upset your friend too.

Wait. Continue to be friendly, but wait two or three weeks before you offer another invitation. Give your friend a chance to invite you over to their house. That way, your new friendship is something you're building together.

NOW YOU TRY IT!

It takes courage to Reach Out to other kids to start a friendship, but think how good you feel when someone smiles at you, gives you a compliment, or invites you to do something. Someone is waiting to be your friend. Who will it be? Are you brave enough to find that person? Here are some questions to help you think more about Reaching Out to make friends.

* What interests do you have that could build Common Ground with other kids? What are some new activities you'd like to try that kids you know enjoy doing?

* Who would you like to compliment? What could you say? Try offering a sincere compliment to five different people this week.

* Have you ever had the experience of having or being an Octopus Friend? What was that like? What do you think you could do to fix or prevent that situation?

* Kids often have different kinds of friends connected to different interests or different situations. What different kinds of friends do you have or could you have?

* Think of the kids you know. Who would you like to invite to your home? Can you think of at least three? What fun things could you do with a friend on a play date?

PART II
Stepping Back to Keep Friends

Most kids want to have friends, but sometimes, without meaning to, kids end up doing things that push friends away. Have you ever had someone tell you that you were being annoying? If you have, that's OK so long as you quickly stop doing whatever is bothering the other person. The next three chapters of *Growing Friendships* is about **Stepping Back.** It will help you figure out how to stop—and when you need to stop—so you can keep the friends you make.

4

Notice Stop Signals

AIDAN'S CHALLENGE: TRYING TO BE FUNNY

It's fun to be around people who make us laugh, but humor is tricky. When joking around happens at the wrong time, in the wrong place, in the wrong way, or with the wrong person, it's not funny; it's annoying. That's what's happening with Aidan. He's trying to be funny, but Julia definitely isn't enjoying his humor.

WHEN TRYING TO BE FUNNY DOESN'T WORK

Aidan wants Julia to notice him and smile at him, so he acts silly. He kicks her chair and imitates her. But instead of smiling, Julia gets annoyed. And that's when Aidan makes his mistake bigger: He keeps going and going, hoping that kicking Julia's chair will become funny. The problem is, if something isn't funny the first time, it definitely won't get funnier if you do it again and again. Aidan needs to learn to Step Back.

Stepping Back means being able to stop doing something that others find annoying. It's an important part of friendship because if you keep annoying people, they won't want to be around you.

To Step Back, you need to notice *Stop Signals.* Sometimes people tell you with their words that they want you to stop. They might make a polite request or an angry demand. Sometimes they tell you with their face or body. They might roll their eyes, frown, cross their arms, or turn away. You need to listen to all of these clues or that person might get very mad at you. If you ignore Stop Signals, other people think you don't care about their feelings.

FIGURE IT OUT

Can you find the Stop Signals in these sentences?

a. Quit it!

b. What time is it?

c. My sister has brown eyes.

d. Cut it out!

e. You're being annoying!

f. No, I'm in fourth grade, not third.

g. Please don't call me that.

h. Be quiet.

Answers: *a, d, e, g,* and *h.* Although *f* has the word "no" in it, it's a clarification, not a Stop Signal.

Sometimes when people try to be funny, they don't just annoy others; they also end up hurting someone's feelings. Then they make the situation worse by saying, "I was just kidding! Can't you take a joke?" This makes the other person even more upset.

SAYING SORRY WHEN YOU BOTHER SOMEONE

If your comments or actions are annoying or upsetting someone, you need to stop right away. Start by saying, "Sorry!" That shows you understand that you were bothering the other person and you care enough to stop. After that, it may help to sit on your hands, cross your legs, or pretend that your tongue is stuck to the roof of your mouth to prevent yourself from doing the annoying action. You may also want to step away for a while to let the other person stop feeling annoyed.

Everybody makes **social mistakes** sometimes. We might tell a joke that people don't think is funny or a story that others don't find interesting. That's OK as long as we listen to Stop Signals.

Humor can be risky, especially with people we don't know well. Instead of trying to be funny, a more sure-fire friendship strategy is to be kind. It's very hard to mess up kindness.

Aidan, the boy at the beginning of this chapter, was annoying other kids by trying to be funny, but that's not the only kind of behavior that can be annoying. Too much arguing can also lead to Stop Signals.

Have you ever had a **Yes-No Argument** with a friend? It sounds like this:

Yes-No Arguments

In a Yes-No Argument, the words just go back and forth, but no one is listening and nothing is getting solved. The angry faces and hands on hips are clear Stop Signals, but the kids just keep annoying each other and getting louder and louder.

When you're feeling angry, it's tempting to yell. Maybe you think that if you make your point louder, you will convince your friend you're right. But more volume is *not* more convincing. There is no way your friend will say, "Ah, now that you've said that more loudly, I agree with you!" In fact, your friend's reaction to yelling is likely to be the opposite of what you want.

The louder you yell, the harder it is for people to hear you. Can you explain why?

When you yell, people don't want to listen to you. It hurts their ears. Yelling at people is mean, and it can be scary. They'll probably just tell you to be quiet, or they might yell back at *you* even louder.

What can you do to respond to Stop Signals and Step Back from an argument with a friend? Here are some possibilities:

EXPLAIN

Try telling your friend clearly and calmly why you think the way you do. This way, maybe your friend will understand and agree with you, or maybe you can find a Compromise. (We'll talk about Compromising in chapter 10.)

ASK

Ask your friend to explain to you what she's thinking. You could say, "What do you want to do?" or "What do you like about that?" or "What don't you like about that?" When you understand what your friend wants, you're better able to figure out how to move forward. Use the words *what* or *how* rather than *why* because *why* can sound like you're scolding. "Why in the world would you want to do that?!" is not a kind question.

AGREE TO DISAGREE

No two people are ever going to agree all the time. Sometimes you just have to accept that and move past it. You could tell your friend, "OK, I guess we just see things differently about that." Then change the subject.

GIVE IN

This is a hard one—especially when you're sure you're right and your friend is wrong. You don't have to give in all the time, but sometimes, just out of caring for your friend, you can say, "OK, we'll do it your way." Sometimes it's more important to be kind than to be fair.

If you tend to get into a lot of arguments with your friend, this friendship probably won't last unless the two of you figure out some ways to be together more peacefully. You have the choice to Step Back from arguments by Explaining, Asking, Agreeing to Disagree, or Giving In. When you do this, you show how much you care for your friend and you make it more comfortable for your friend to be with you.

5

Give the Benefit of the Doubt

SUSAN'S CHALLENGE: ASSUMING MEANNESS

People who get angry a lot assume that other people do things out of deliberate meanness. Susan didn't know what the girls were talking about, but she immediately jumped to the conclusion that they were saying something bad about her.

It's an act of kindness to **Believe the Best** about people. That means understanding that most people are kind, most of the time. For example, in this last cartoon, there are a lot of non-mean reasons why the girls might have been whispering:

* Maybe the girls were talking about something that had nothing to do with Susan.

* Maybe they were saying something about themselves that was embarrassing so they wanted to keep it private.

* Maybe they didn't realize Susan was nearby, and they would have included her in their conversation if they'd seen her.

* Maybe they were actually saying something nice about her!

Believing the Best makes it possible for Susan to keep her friendship with them. If Susan keeps asking and accusing, "Were you talking about me? Why were you talking about me? I know you were talking about me!" she will annoy the girls and actually give them something to talk about! It's not good manners to whisper in front of others, but it's not Susan's job to correct them. Also, it's kind of conceited if Susan assumes that she's so incredibly interesting that other kids talk about her all the time.

THEY'RE PROBABLY NOT TRYING TO BE MEAN

It's pretty rare for kids—especially friends—to be mean on purpose. Most of the time when they do something you don't like, it's an accident or a misunderstanding or they just didn't realize it would upset you. Considering explanations *other than* deliberate meanness can help you avoid overreacting.

The Maybe Game involves thinking of possible non-mean reasons why someone might have done something you didn't like. Here are some examples:

Maybe John thought it was his.

Maybe he picked it up to return it to you later.

Can you think of another non-mean reason to explain what John did?

Maybe Dora couldn't find you.

Maybe she hadn't played with her other friend in a long time and that friend missed her.

Can you think of another non-mean reason to explain what Dora did?

45

But what if the girls in the cartoon at the start of this chapter really *were* saying something mean about Susan? What if she actually heard them say something like, "Susan is so stuck up!" Should she confront them? Probably not. They'll just deny it or get mad at her for accusing them. If the girls aren't talking directly to Susan, then Susan doesn't have to respond to them in any way.

It's hard to accept, but the fact is, we can't control what other people say about us. We can't tape their mouths shut!

Demanding that others stop talking about you fuels gossip. It gives kids even more to whisper about. Often the best thing to do is to pretend the gossip doesn't bother you and let the mean comments fade. This is very hard to do! You may feel upset inside, but you don't want to show how you feel to the gossipers because seeing you hurt or angry makes them feel powerful. It may help to remember that the people who know and care about you won't believe the bad things people say and will like you anyway.

If you find that certain people often say mean things about you, it may be a sign that you should try to hang out with kinder friends.

46

6
Handle Stressful Situations

KYLE'S CHALLENGE: CRYING EASILY

Kyle is very upset that he didn't spell his word right in the spelling bee. Anyone in that situation would feel disappointed and maybe even embarrassed. But Kyle becomes so upset that he cries.

CRYING TOO OFTEN

Everyone cries sometimes. If you're feeling very sad, disappointed, or hurt, sometimes tears just seem to well up, and that's OK. The problem in Kyle's situation is that he is crying often about things that don't make other kids cry, and he's doing it in front of the whole class. Did you notice how the girl told the teacher, "Kyle is crying again"? When tears become a habit, they can push other kids away.

Kids want to be around kids who are happy and having fun. They might respond in caring ways the first time you cry, but their sympathy will dry up if you cry often. Also, some kids tend to pick on kids who cry easily. Unfortunately, if you're older than kindergarten, crying a lot in public can make you seem babyish to others.

Having a habit of crying won't help you make or keep friends, and it makes you feel more unhappy overall. If you're spending a lot of time crying, you're not spending that time learning or playing with your friends or doing other fun and interesting things.

Maybe you feel like you can't help crying, but there are some **Emergency Calming Strategies** that you can use to ease your upset and make it less likely that your tears will flow in public. After you're feeling calmer, then you can think through how to handle the situation.

EMERGENCY CALMING STRATEGIES

Breathe slowly and silently. Breathe in for five seconds (count the seconds in your head: "One-one thousand, two-one thousand . . .), hold your breath for five seconds, and then gently breathe out for five seconds. Keep doing this until you feel more settled and in control of your emotions.

Distract yourself. Concentrating on something else. Look out the window, count ceiling tiles, do math facts in your head, or make a mental list of all your relatives or the kids in your class.

Take a break. Sometimes it helps to step away from the situation. You could get a drink of water or take a short trip to the bathroom and imagine yourself rinsing away the upset as you wash your hands.

COMFORT YOURSELF

Even better than using an Emergency Calming Strategy when bad things happen is to try not to get too upset in the first place. The way we talk to ourselves in our heads affects how we feel. When Kyle got his word wrong and had to sit down in the spelling bee, he was probably thinking things like this:

This is not a kind way for Kyle to talk to himself. These thoughts also make him feel more and more upset. No one likes to lose, but the way Kyle is talking to himself makes the situation feel much worse and much bigger than it really is.

Imagine that you're Kyle's friend. What would you say to comfort him? Maybe you'd say something like, "It's OK. That was a hard word," or "Maybe you just need some extra practice," or even "Everybody messes up sometimes."

If you know how to comfort a friend, you know how to comfort yourself. Treat yourself the way you would treat a friend. You would never say to a friend, "You're such a loser!" but sometimes that's the way kids talk to themselves. It's mean, it doesn't help, and it just gets you more upset. Don't be mean to yourself!

USE COPING THOUGHTS

In addition to comforting yourself, coping thoughts can help you handle a tough situation. You can't trick yourself by saying, "This is great!" when it isn't, but you *can* give yourself a little pep talk. You could say something like, "I don't like this, but I'll get through it," or "I've dealt with hard things before," or "It won't last long," or "I'm strong enough to handle this." Most of the time, bad events are just a bump in the road of life and you can get past them.

Here are some examples of kids who are talking meanly to themselves. Think of some things to say that would make them feel better.

Oh no! I did horribly on this test! I'm so stupid!

What could you say to help this girl feel better? One possibility is, "You're not stupid. It was a hard test. Maybe you can talk to the teacher so you'll understand things better."

What could you say to help the boy in the cartoon above feel better? One idea is, "Jared is always nice to you when he sees you, so he doesn't hate you. He probably just wants to have more than one friend. Maybe you could try being friends with Tony too."

The next time something bad happens to you, remember to talk to yourself in kind ways. Be a good friend to yourself!

MOVING AWAY FROM BAD FEELINGS

It's normal to feel sad or angry when something bad happens, but we don't want to get stuck on those feelings. At some point (sooner is better than later!) you need to decide, "I'm going to move on. I'm not going to let these feelings hold me back any longer." When you start acting as if you feel better, you'll probably find that the painful feelings will fade.

Sometimes moving on means taking action so things will go better next time. For instance, Kyle could get his mom or dad to quiz him so he feels more confident at the next spelling bee. Sometimes there's nothing you can do to change the bad event, so you just need to step away from the upsetting thoughts or memories and do something pleasant to be kind to yourself. Maybe you could shoot some hoops with a friend, cook dinner with your mom or dad, listen to music, or read a favorite book. What helps you feel better when you're upset?

NOW YOU TRY IT!

We've talked about a lot of different situations where kids need to Step Back to keep friends. These include noticing Stop Signals to avoid annoying people with humor that misses the mark, Believing the Best about friends instead of unfairly getting angry at them, and resisting the urge to cry in public so we're ready and able to enjoy being with friends. If we barrel through, ignoring other people's reactions, we end up pushing them away.

Stepping Back is not an easy thing to do, but it's important because it's a way of caring for others and yourself. The key to Stepping Back is being aware of how others are reacting to us. Are they smiling or annoyed? Are they moving toward or away from us? These responses give us clues about whether we might need to stop what we're doing or do something different. Here are some questions to help you think more about Stepping Back to keep friends:

* How can you tell if you're doing friendly teasing versus teasing that goes too far and ends up annoying people or hurting someone's feelings? (Hint: Look for clues in how others react. What would you see in each case?)

* Why does it not help to say, "Just kidding!" after you've annoyed or upset someone? What's a better way to respond?

* What are some things you can do when you feel angry to help yourself calm down?

* Think of a disagreement you had with a friend. How did you try to solve it? What, if anything, could you do differently next time to prevent or solve the problem?

* Why is it not a good idea to get upset in front of people you don't know? What can you do if you feel like crying in public?

* Is there a situation where you tend to talk meanly to yourself? What could you say instead? What comforting thing would you say to a friend in that situation? Maybe that would be a good thing to say to yourself.

PART III
Blending In to Join Friends

One-on-one friendships are great, but being part of a group of friends can multiply your fun. Have you ever heard the saying "The more the merrier"? When more people are involved, there are more ideas, more excitement, and more laughter. But more opinions can also make it harder to play or work together. Have you ever felt like an outsider while others look like they're having a great time together? Have you ever been part of a group project or sports team where you've felt frustrated because people didn't cooperate? This part of *Growing Friendships* talks about **Blending In.** It will help you figure out how to join a group, get along with partners or teammates, and contribute to the group's fun.

7

Join the Fun

**MACKENZIE'S CHALLENGE:
STANDING ON THE SIDELINES**

Mackenzie is watching the other girls have fun, and she wishes she could join in, but she feels like she can't because they haven't specifically invited her to play with them. Does this mean the other girls don't like her or don't want her to play with them? Probably not. They may be so involved in all that splashing, jumping, and swimming that they don't notice her. Or maybe they think *she* doesn't want to play with *them* because she's staying away from them.

What should Mackenzie do to join the group? Should she walk up to the girls and ask to play?

Well-meaning grown-ups might suggest this because it seems sensible and polite, and it's what grown-ups tend to do, but it's usually *not* a good idea for kids to ask to join a group of kids.

If Mackenzie asks, "Can I play too?" she'll interrupt the play. They will have to stop what they're doing, turn around and look at her, and decide whether they want her to join. Asking to join also gives jokesters a chance to say, "No! You can't play! Ha ha ha!"

In general, you don't want to draw attention to yourself when you're trying to join a group. There's a better way to do it.

Sometimes it's nice to play by yourself. But I love the excitement of running through the neighborhood with my pack of dog friends. We run so fast saliva flies off our tongues!

Cats prefer activities that don't involve drool.

THE SECRET TO JOINING A GROUP

Have you ever watched your grown-ups drive onto a highway? First they watch the traffic, and then they slide into it without interrupting the flow. In driving this is called merging, but when it comes to making friends, we call it **Watch Then Blend.**

What would happen if your grown-ups just barged into the traffic flow without looking? Yep, there'd be a big crash! Just barging in doesn't work with kids, either. If Mackenzie had suddenly jumped into the pool on top of the other girls, they probably would have gotten mad at her for interrupting them. On the other hand just watching and waiting without joining doesn't get kids (or cars) anywhere.

PUTTING WATCH THEN BLEND INTO ACTION

Joining a group of kids is just like drivers merging onto a highway. All you have to do is Watch Then Blend. This means:

1. Stand near a group and watch what they are doing; then

2. Slide into the action without interrupting it.

How exactly do you use the Watch Then Blend strategy? First you need to watch closely so you understand how the group is playing or what they're trying to do. Then you do something that adds to the play. Here are some possible ways to Blend:

* Do the same thing the group is doing nearby; then gradually move closer.

* Give a compliment.

* Bring extra toys or supplies.

* Help them lift, carry, or get something so they can continue the play.

* Get in line to take a turn.

Isn't it rude to join without asking? No. Just the opposite: it's respectful of the ongoing play to contribute without interrupting the flow.

Here's an example of how Mackenzie could Watch Then Blend with the girls at the pool. Notice how she first watches to understand what they're doing and then uses a compliment to get closer. Then she finally joins in by doing what they are doing and adding to the fun without interrupting the flow.

Watch . . .

Then Blend . . .

To Join

What if the other girls won't let Mackenzie join them? What if they tell her it's a private game? It can happen. Even well-liked kids get left out sometimes. But if Mackenzie doesn't try to join at all, she's guaranteed not to be part of the fun.

You're most likely to be able to join either one kid playing alone or a group of four or more. If you're not already good friends with them, groups of two or three can be very close knit, which makes them harder to join.

JOINING A GAME WITH RULES

So far we've been talking about how to join a group of kids who are just hanging out and playing. But how do you join a game with rules? If it's a short game or a two-player game, just watch and wait until it's finished and join in the next round. You could say, "I'll play the winner!"

If a group is playing a sport, you can stand close by when they're picking teams. Or, if one team has fewer players, you could join the smaller team to make the teams more even.

If a game is already going on, try to join the *losing* team. The losing team will be more open than the winning team to having your help. Wait for a break in the action and then do something that keeps the game moving. For instance, you could run to get a ball that goes out of bounds and then join the team.

THE RIGHT WAY AND THE WRONG WAY TO JOIN A GROUP

On the next pages are some more examples of trying to join a group. Can you tell which ones are the right way and which are the wrong way?

Did you guess the second cartoon? That way of joining is more respectful and is a good example of Watch Then Blend.

Did you guess the second cartoon again? In the first one, the girl might think she's being funny, but she's actually barging in. In the second cartoon, she joins by helping.

NO ROOM IN THE GAME?

If you try to blend into a group and the other kids won't let you play, don't push it. Becoming angry or demanding won't help your cause and it's likely to make the group more determined to keep you out. Just walk away calmly with a pleasant look on your face (even if you're not feeling pleasant!). You can try joining another group or just wait and try again later with the first group.

If a particular group won't let you join two or three times, don't keep trying. Find another group that will include you. And if the people in a group let you join but then are mean to you, leave and definitely look for a different group.

CHOOSING WHICH GROUP TO JOIN

How do you decide which group to join? Try to be friendly with everyone around your age. If you're in a new situation with kids you know only a little bit, it's a good idea to smile and be near them. For instance, if you just started a new soccer team and you recognize some kids from your school, you should definitely say hi and stand next to them for the warm-up exercises.

It's just good manners to say hi to people you know. This is a good first step to joining. A friendship might grow from there, or it might not, but you don't want to kill the possibility of friendship by staying away from the start. Acting as if you don't know someone comes across as unfriendly.

What about people you *do* know well? How do you decide whether you should join a certain friendship group? Here are some questions to consider:

* Do you like doing the same things these kids do?

* Have the group members shown signs that they enjoy your company? (For instance, do they smile when they see you or include you when they make plans?)

* Do you feel good when you're with them?

* Do you have fun together?

* Are they usually kind to you?

* Do your parents and teacher seem to like them?

If you answered no to any of these questions, joining that group may not be a good choice for you. Sometimes kids stick with a group of "friends" who are often mean to them because they think they don't have any other choice. But there's always another choice! It's hard to move away from a familiar group, but it's better to do that than to allow yourself to be treated badly again and again.

Sometimes kids choose to hang out with groups of kids who get in trouble a lot. That's not good, either. If you hang out with kids who are troublemakers, people might think you're a troublemaker too.

You don't have to belong to just one group. Having more than one circle of friends is fun and interesting. It gives you more options and allows you to do different things with different friends. For instance, you might enjoy playing sports with one group of friends and having good conversations with another and doing school projects with a third group.

My owner doesn't like it when I hang out with the Siamese cats next door because they like to pee on the couch. But it's my couch, so then I have to pee on it too. And then they pee some more, so I have to pee more . . .

That sounds like a very wet play date.

CHANGING FRIENDSHIP GROUPS

Sometimes interests or situations change and people end up switching friendship groups. They may start spending more time with one group and less time with another. That's normal.

It's hard if you're the one being left behind when your buddy shifts friendship groups, but clinging and arguing will just push your friend away more. You may want to try to join your friend's new group. Or you could use the shift to start spending more time with a different group. If you stay on good terms, you may find that your friend shifts back to your group after a while.

If you're the one moving away from an old group of friends, try not to be mean about it. Don't criticize your old group or announce, "I don't like you anymore!" Be sure to say only good things about your old group to the new group.

Try to stay friendly with your old group while building your connection to the new group. If you make an effort to get together with your old group sometimes, you can still be friends with them, even if you're spending less time together. Also, if the new group turns out to be not as nice as you thought, you'll still have friends to play with if you stay connected with your old group.

8
Match the Tone

There is no possibility of the other boys responding well to Jason's comments. He probably thinks that he has better taste in books than they do, and that's why he feels he needs to share his opinion. But his comments come across as a criticism of the other boys. It's almost like he's shouting, "I'M NOT PART OF THIS GROUP!!!"

But isn't he allowed to have his own opinion about the books? Of course he is.

Does he have to like this series just because everybody else does? Definitely not.

Should he lie and say he likes them, when he really doesn't, just to fit in? No. Lying or being fake is never a good basis for a friendship!

But here's the problem: he can't join a group by disrupting the feeling of their conversation. If he wants to join this particular group, he has to **Match the Tone** of their comments. This means he needs to pick up on the feeling of the conversation and say something that has a similar feeling.

CONTRIBUTE TO THE CONVERSATION

A conversation is like a song. Each person in the conversation adds to the music. When someone says something that doesn't fit with the general feeling of the conversation, it's like a jarring wrong note. It disrupts the conversation.

MATCH THE TONE

In the conversation at the start of this chapter, the general feeling is enthusiasm and excitement about the book. To join this conversation, Jason needs to say something enthusiastic. He shouldn't lie. He doesn't have to say he liked the book when he doesn't, but he does have to match the feeling. For instance, instead of criticizing the book that

the other boys clearly enjoyed, he could ask what the book is about or he could ask them if they've read another funny book he likes.

If Jason wanted to join another group where they were all saying negative things about this book series, then his comment about them being babyish wouldn't seem out of place.

Matching the Tone of a conversation doesn't mean you have to turn into an exact copy of other kids in order to have friends. Sometimes friends disagree, and that's OK. But it's polite to figure out the feeling of the conversation and make only comments that match it so you don't disrupt the discussion.

In these cartoon conversations, can you figure out which final comment would fit best with the general feeling?

Comment 1

Comment 2

Did you guess the second comment? That's correct! But what if you really did think the test was easy? Do you have to pretend you're dumb just to fit in? No. The boy in the second cartoon didn't lie and say he thought the test was hard, but he did say something honest that matched the feeling of the other boys' comments.

On the other hand, the comment by the boy in the first cartoon is a put-down. He's implying that he's better than the other boys, and that's no way to join a group.

Comment 1

Comment 2

Did you guess the second comment again? That's correct! But what if you hate, hate, hate the color pink? That's fine, but you don't have to share that opinion when you know someone disagrees with you. Calling someone else's taste stupid, makes it seem like you're calling that person stupid. That's not kind.

9

Contribute to the Team

CARLOS'S CHALLENGE: AFRAID OF NOT BEING THE BEST

Carlos enjoys playing baseball, but he only wants to do it if he knows he'll be one of the best kids on his team. Maybe he's afraid he'll feel embarrassed when the older boys play better than he does. Maybe he's afraid the older boys will make fun of him. Carlos is missing the point of being part of a team.

A team is a group of people *working together* toward some goal. That's called cooperation or teamwork. Everyone pitches in to help the whole team.

Think of your favorite sports team. Does it have only one player on it? Does that player always perform perfectly? Of course not. Even the best players have bad games. Professional baseball players only get a hit about one-third of the time! Star players need the other players to help them do their best, and sometimes it's a junior member of the team who saves the day. Different players have different strengths, and everyone on a team plays an important role.

83

Carlos's attitude of "If I'm not the best, then I quit" shows that he's more focused on comparing himself to others than on what he can do for the team. If he cared about the team, he'd be thinking, "I'm going to work very hard at every practice so I can get better and help us win!" Teamwork involves asking yourself, "What can I give?" rather than "How am I doing?"

Carlos also needs to understand that there are many ways to contribute to a team. Performing well is only one type of contribution. Even if he's not the best batter or fielder, he could do a very good job of being encouraging when his teammates mess up, cheering loudly when they do well, trying hard so that everyone feels motivated, or just being cheerful and fun to be around. The best part of being on a team is just having fun together.

Sports teams are one kind of team, but there are lots of others. A family can be a team. Friends or classmates can also be a team when they cooperate and support each other. Take a look at these examples of teams in the following cartoons. Have you ever been part of a team?

FIGURE IT OUT

Anything that helps people work well together contributes to a team and shows cooperation. Here's a list of some actions by people on different types of teams. Can you tell which ones make the team stronger?

a. When Maureen makes a suggestion at robotics club, Nishta says, "That's a stupid idea! It'll never work!"

b. Jakob helps pick up after chess club, even if he didn't make the mess.

c. Morgan yells at Tricia for missing a goal in soccer.

d. After she loses in a family game of charades, Sanjay tells his little sister, "Nice try! You're getting better at this!"

e. Emilie works hard on her part of the project on insects and makes sure she gets it done on time.

f. James cracks jokes at hockey practice.

Answers: *b*, *d*, and *e* all help teammates work happily together. *f* could go either way. Laughing together helps teammates enjoy each other's company, but if James gets too silly, he could interfere with the team following the coach's directions.

NOW YOU TRY IT!

Blending In with a group can be harder than hanging out with just one friend, but group activities can be especially fun. It's also a skill that you'll use your whole life. Blending In doesn't mean you have to be exactly the same as everyone else or be a follower. It's about understanding and respecting other people's point of view so you can do things together, like play a game or have a good conversation. Blending In means being aware of how your actions fit with other people's goals and feelings so you can all cooperate!

* What groups do you belong to now? (Hint: think of clubs, teams, and family or friendship groups.) What could you do to contribute to the teamwork in those groups?

* What group do you think you'd like to join? What do you like about that group? How could you start Blending In with them?

* Have you or someone you know ever changed friendship groups? Why? What happened?

* Why is it a good idea to match the emotional tone of a conversation? How would you feel if you were excited about something and your friend responded with complaining comments? Would it be harder or easier than if you were feeling upset about something and your friend responded with excited comments?

PART IV
Speaking Up to Share with Friends

Speaking up, huh? Does that mean Speaking up in front of a crowd of cheering fans? I'd really like to have a fan club. You know, a big group of people who get together to talk about how long and lovely my whiskers are. Does it say anything about how to get a fan club?

I'd be surprised if that's what this part of the book is about.

Good friends tell each other about what they're thinking and feeling. That's how they get to know each other better. But it's not always easy to get your point across. You may have trouble saying what you think or feel because you worry that others won't like it. But if you don't say anything, your friends won't understand what you want.

Maybe you sometimes share your thoughts and feelings too strongly. Yelling, calling people names, or crying easily might be honest reactions, but they could end up pushing friends away.

This part of *Growing Friendships* is about **Speaking Up** to say what you mean without being mean. It's about *what* you say and *how* you say it.

10

Be True to Yourself

CHRISTOPHER'S CHALLENGE: NOT SHARING WHAT HE THINKS

Christopher thinks he's being nice to Josh by not disagreeing with him. It's good that Christopher cares about how Josh feels. It's *not* good that he didn't give Josh a chance to care about Christopher's feelings.

Christopher is actually being very unfair to Josh. He's mad at Josh for preventing him from playing tag, but how could Josh know that he wanted to play tag if Christopher never told him? It's not fair to be mad at someone for failing to read our minds!

A good way to handle a disagreement with a friend

93

is to offer a ***Compromise.*** A Compromise means doing partly what you want and partly what your friend wants. Here are some different ways that Christopher could have Compromised with Josh.

Compromise 1

Compromise 2

Either of these solutions would have been better than Christopher giving in while being silently resentful or angry at Josh. Christopher was worried about Josh getting mad at him, but his choice to say nothing made him mad at Josh.

Speaking Up means finding that tone that is just right—not too soft and not too hard—to express your thoughts and feelings. If your words are too soft, your friends won't know what you want. That's not respectful of yourself. If your words are too hard, your friends will feel like you don't care about them. That's not respectful of them.

USING THE RIGHT TONE

One way to get that just-right tone is to use *"I" Statements.* "I" Statements are comments that begin with the word "I" and describe what you think, feel, or want without criticizing someone else.

Making "I" Statements can solve problems by helping friends talk about disagreements without blaming each other. When you start with "I," you are giving your point of view while recognizing that your friend might see things differently.

Instead of . . .

Try . . .

Instead of . . .

Try . . .

After you make an "I" Statement, you can follow up with a polite request, such as, "Could you please move your foot?" or you could suggest a Compromise such as, "How about if we both move our chairs over a little bit?"

Here is an example of a conversation between friends. Have you ever been in a situation like this?

HANNAH AND HER FRIEND'S HAIRCUT

In the last box of this cartoon, is Hannah being too soft or too hard? If you guessed "too hard," you're right! Hannah's comments are not respectful of her friend. They will definitely make her friend feel bad. Hannah just blurted out her thoughts without considering how her words would affect her friend. This is called having no Filter, and it can be very hurtful to others. A *Filter* is something that lets some things pass through and holds other things back. As much as we can, we want to Filter our words so that only kind ones come through.

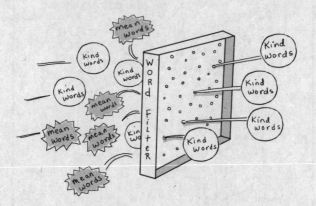

But what if the haircut really does look bad? Should Hannah lie and say it looks good? No. Good friends are honest with each other. If the friend doesn't ask, Hannah doesn't have to say anything, but if the friend does ask, she can find a kind way to share her opinion.

Here's another conversation between friends. What would you say in this situation?

MARTIN'S CARDS

In the last box of this cartoon, is Martin being too soft or too hard? If you guessed "too soft," you're right. Why is Martin apologizing when he didn't do anything wrong? That's not being respectful of himself. If you make a mistake, of course you should apologize. A sincere apology when you mess up is a good way to resolve a problem with friends. But some kids apologize many times for no reason. They think they are being extra nice, but they're really putting themselves down. It's like they're saying, "It's my fault anytime anything anywhere in the world goes wrong!" This is not true. It's also a bit annoying for others to hear "I'm sorry" again and again.

Martin cares a lot about his collection. He doesn't like the cards being dumped out. If he doesn't explain this to his friend, he's not being respectful of himself and it could end the friendship. He either needs to explain to his friend how he wants his cards or never have the friend over again. Explaining is the kinder thing to do.

Yelling at the other boy and saying something like, "You jerk! You wrecked everything! I hate you!" would not go over well. The other boy wasn't trying to be mean. He just got excited, and he didn't realize that the cards were arranged in a particular order. He would feel unfairly attacked if Martin yelled at him, and he wouldn't want to stay friends with Martin.

What could Martin say that's not too soft and not too hard? He could try an "I" Statement plus a polite request.

Making an "I" Statement and a polite request takes courage on Martin's part, but it gives the other boy a chance to respond in a caring way. Speaking Up kindly makes it possible for the boys to get past this difficult moment and understand each other better.

11

Say No When Needed

MARLA'S CHALLENGE: GIVING IN TOO MUCH

Why did Marla agree to give away her cookies? Probably she thought she had to do it! Maybe she didn't want to seem mean. Maybe she didn't want the other girl to be mad at her. But Marla ended up feeling mad instead. Marla doesn't want to give away her cookies, but she does it anyway, so she's not being respectful of herself.

Sharing with friends is a kind thing to do, but it should be something you do willingly, when you want to, not something you feel pressured into doing. Just because the other girl asks doesn't mean that Marla has to give away her cookies. If she is feeling very generous and the girl is a close friend, Marla could offer to give her one of her cookies, but she doesn't *have* to do that. It's her lunch and her treat.

What should Marla have said in this situation? Here's one possibility:

This might be a hard thing for Marla to say, but it's important if she wants to stay friends with the other girl. Otherwise, Marla will walk away from lunch feeling angry at the other girl, and the girl will have no idea why.

What about Marla's friend? Was she being mean by suggesting the trade? No. It's OK for her to ask. It's Marla's job to figure out if she feels comfortable with the trade. Of course, if Marla says no, the girl needs to accept that without arguing.

Saying no to someone is one of the hardest types of Speaking Up. Sometimes you have to say no more than once before some people will listen to you. Here are a few different ways to say no. Which ones seem most comfortable to you?

WAYS TO SAY NO

"No, thanks."

"I'm not comfortable doing that."

"That's just not my kind of thing to do."

"My mom would be so mad if I did that!"

"I don't want to do that. Let's do something else instead."

"I don't like that idea."

"I really don't want to do that."

"I don't feel like doing that."

Try practicing some of these ways to say no in the following cartoons. The other person is going to ask three times, so you'll need to say no three times! Remember, you don't have to yell to get your point across. Just say no calmly and confidently.

Ooh! You definitely need to say no to letting someone copy your homework or you might get in trouble for cheating. Giving answers counts as cheating as much as taking answers. Which of the **Ways to Say No** could you use now? Pick one from the list on the previous page or come up with your own.

Come on! No one will find out.

Yikes! He's still asking! You're going to have to say no again! Which "No" could you say now?

Friends are supposed to help each other. If you were really my friend you would give me the answers.

Wow! He's really being persistent! But that's OK. You know lots of ways to say no. Try a different one!

Here's another situation where you need to say no. How would you handle it?

This friend wants you to join her in being mean to Carmela. That's not the right thing to do, so you need to say no. Which of the *Ways to Say No* would you use?

Carmela and I had a big fight. She's so mean. I'm not going to talk to her anymore. Promise me you won't talk to her either!

Well, if you were really my friend, you'd be on my side. Don't talk to her!

She's pushing you hard, but you need to be true to what you know is right. Tell her no again.

This is a tough situation. Your friend is feeling hurt and angry, but joining her in being mean to Carmela is not the right thing to do. Two against one is not fair, and it's unkind to refuse to speak to someone. You can sympathize with your friend but you don't have to join her in being mean to Carmela. Which of the *Ways to Say No* could you say now? Stand your ground and tell her no without yelling.

Saying no can be very difficult, especially when you have to do it several times, but it gets easier with practice. If you're not sure whether you want to say no or OK, you can usually take some time to think things over. Tell your friend, "I need to think about that. I'll let you know later." Then make sure you get back to your friend with your decision. If you say no, your friend can make other plans. If you don't answer, your friend is stuck waiting for your decision.

12
Handle Teasing and Bullying

PAUL'S CHALLENGE: OVERREACTING TO SILLINESS

Paul is Speaking Up in a way that is too hard. He accuses Conrad of being a bully and wants to end their friendship over a single comment. It's true that Conrad laughing at Paul's initials is not very nice, but is it really Bullying?

No. Conrad is not trying to be mean. He's just fooling around and being silly. He likes Paul and isn't trying to hurt or upset him. For Conrad, the teasing is playful, but Paul doesn't understand this.

If you get picked on, the first thing you need to do is figure out what kind of teasing it is. There are three main kinds of teasing:

1. Teasing between friends

2. Teasing between Non-friends

3. Bullying.

Deciding which of these is happening in your situation is important because you need to handle them differently. It can be hard telling these apart, so let's take a closer look at each of these.

IS IT REALLY BULLYING?

Just because someone does something that upsets you doesn't mean they are Bullying you. Teasing between friends is often a sign of playfulness and affection. Bullying is much different.

Bullying is *deliberate act* of meanness, aimed at a *specific person*, that's often *repeated over time*. It only counts as Bullying if the person is *trying* to hurt or upset you.

One more very important thing about Bullying is that it involves a **Power Difference**. A Power Difference means that the kid doing the Bullying is somehow more powerful than the kid getting bullied. In other words, the one doing the Bullying is bigger, older, stronger, tougher, or much more popular. This Power Difference is what makes it hard for kids who are bullied to defend or protect themselves.

Sometimes Bullying is physical and can include hitting, pushing, or kicking. Sometimes it involves mean words such as insulting someone, spreading rumors, or trying to get people to exclude someone. Sometimes Bullying even happens online. This is called cyberbullying. All the different forms of Bullying are about hurting someone weaker on purpose.

This is Bullying

This is Bullying

This is **not** Bullying because there's no Power Difference

115

If the kids involved are equals, then it's *not* Bullying. It's just a conflict, mistake, or misunderstanding. Those are things that kids can learn to handle on their own.

FIGURE IT OUT

In these examples, can you tell which ones are *not* Bullying?

a. Jordan decides to sit with Vijay instead of Sam on the bus today.

b. Marisol tells Kiley not to play with Shana because Shana wears ugly clothes.

c. Juan and Parker tell Max that if he tries to go on the slide, they'll push him off.

d. Stuart deliberately trips Keisha so she'll drop her lunch.

e. Rachel puts an unsigned note in Kim's backpack that says, "Nobody likes you."

f. Norita invites Jennifer over for a play date but doesn't invite Michelle.

g. Nihal beats Brian at checkers three times in a row.

h. Every time they play an online game, Kevin tells all the boys to gang up on Vinnie.

Answers: *a*, *f*, and *g* might be upsetting but they are not Bullying because they don't involve deliberate meanness. They are just normal Friendship Rough Spots.

We'll talk about how to handle Bullying later in this chapter. First let's look at how to handle the milder forms of teasing.

HANDLING FRIENDSHIP ROUGH SPOTS

Every friendship has an occasional *Friendship Rough Spot*. This happens when friends do or say something that unintentionally hurts each other's feelings. If a friendship is mostly good, it's not smart or kind to end it because of a Rough Spot. Instead, you should either accept and move past that bad moment or talk to your friend about it.

In the cartoon at the start of this chapter, Conrad and Paul are friends. Conrad is not more powerful than Paul, so even though Conrad's teasing upset Paul, it's not Bullying. It's just a Friendship Rough Spot. Here are some ways Paul could have responded that wouldn't have involved ending the friendship or calling his friend a bully.

Choice 1: Play it cool.

Choice 2: Play along.

Choice 3: Ask nicely.

Because they are friends, Conrad will probably listen if Paul asks him to stop joking about his initials, but Paul may need to say it more than once to help Conrad understand he's serious. He could say, "I mean it. I really don't think that's funny. Please stop."

HANDLING TEASING BETWEEN NON-FRIENDS

In between friendly teasing and real Bullying is a middle category: *Teasing between **Non-friends***. Non-friends are kids who don't know each other well and don't particularly like each other. Teasing between Non-friends can be mean, but it only crosses the line to become Bullying if there's a Power Difference.

When you are teased by a Non-friend, you need to think about the person who is doing it. This person is not a friend. This is not someone who cares about you, and you don't really care about the teaser, either. You don't need to argue or try to convince the teaser of anything because the teaser's opinion doesn't matter to you.

Don't respond to unkind teasing by showing you are upset. In general, you should only talk about your feelings with people who care about you. If you tell a Non-friend who is being mean to you, "I feel hurt when you say that," then that person might think, "Good! That's what I wanted!"

Non-friends who tease you are trying to push your buttons. Have you ever seen a baby toy that makes funny noises when the baby presses a button? You definitely don't want to be a noisy toy for a Non-friend who is doing mean teasing.

119

If you show a big reaction to teasing—crying, yelling, lashing out, or getting very upset—Non-friend teasers will be entertained. They will see you as an easy target and tease you even more. So you need to Speak Up in a way that tells them their words don't affect you (even if they really do).

You can't stop kids from saying mean things to you. There's also nothing you can say or do that will instantly and permanently stop teasing. But if you avoid overreacting, it's less likely that the teasing will continue.

Show Boredom

How *should* you react to unfriendly teasing? One option is to respond with boredom. In a bored tone, you could say something like one of these comments:

You may want to practice these bored responses by role-playing using *Nonsense Word Insults*. Nonsense Word Insults are silly and pointless phrases. They don't mean anything so they're not upsetting, which makes it easier for you to figure out how to react. Here are some examples of Nonsense Word Insults. See if you can respond to each of them using one of the bored comments above.

You have higgle niffs!

You're such a glip glop!

You always riddly ruck your roops!

Most teasing by Non-friends is just as silly and pointless as these Nonsense Word Insults. If you can handle responding to Nonsense Word Insults with a bored comment, you can handle responding to real teasing the same way. After you make a bored comment to a Non-friend's teasing, walk away. Walking away is important because you shouldn't stick around if someone is being mean to you. If you keep arguing, it will get worse. Walk—don't run—away because you don't want the Non-friend to chase you.

If you can't manage to say anything, just roll your eyes—to show the Non-friend teaser that the comments are ridiculous and so immature—and walk away. (Note: Never do this to an adult!)

Use Humor

Another way to respond to teasing from a Non-friend is with humor. For instance, if someone makes fun of you, you could pretend you're getting a compliment. Say, "Thanks for noticing! You're very observant!" and then simply walk away.

Stay Near Others

A less direct way to deal with teasing from a Non-friend is to stand near a grown-up or a group of your friends. People are less likely to do or say anything mean to you when you are surrounded by people who support you.

Point Out Meanness

What should you do if someone who is in your general circle of friends (but is not really your friend) has a habit of being mean to you? It might help to point out the meanness right when it happens. Say it in a strong, clear voice—not shouting or in an angry tone but loud enough that a grown-up and others can hear. Your tone should be calm and matter-of-fact. In the same way you would announce, "two plus two equals four," say, "That was a mean thing to say." Then walk away.

Most kids don't like to think of themselves as being mean, so pointing out meanness right away could make them think twice about doing it again. You may also get some help from the teacher or other kids.

123

DEALING WITH BULLYING

What if it's more than teasing? What if you're being bullied?

If the meanness keeps happening—even after you've tried responding in some of the ways we've described—that's a more serious situation than just a stray mean comment. If the other kid is tougher or more popular than you are, or if there's a whole group of kids picking on you, you're going to need help.

Maybe someone has told you that you should punch a bully and then the bully will leave you alone. This rarely works. The problem is that if you hit the other kid, that kid is likely to hit you back—harder! Kids who bully usually choose targets who are not as strong as they are.

Should You Tell a Grown-Up?

If you're being bullied, you need to get help from a grown-up. Telling an adult that you're being bullied is *not* tattling because you're reporting a serious and maybe even dangerous situation. You're also standing up for your right to feel safe in your mind and in your body. (We'll talk about tattling in chapter 14.)

How to Tell

Don't announce that you're going to tell an adult. If you yell, "I'm telling!" it will make the person doing the Bullying even madder. Instead, first get away from the situation and then figure out which adults you can talk to about the Bullying. You may want to bring a friend with you for comfort and to back up what you say. When the person doing the Bullying isn't around, explain what's happening to your parents, teacher, or some other trusted adult. It's a good idea to tell the adult how you've already tried to deal with the situation so that the adult understands that this is more than you can handle on your own. It's the adult's job to do what's necessary to keep you safe.

Sometimes kids worry that if they report the Bullying, it will make the situation worse. The kid doing the Bullying may have even threatened to hurt them more if they tell. Tell anyway. It's not OK for anyone to be bullied, including you.

What if the adult doesn't believe you about the Bullying or says something unhelpful like, "Boys will be boys," or "You need to have thicker skin"? Tell someone else. Keep telling until you get an adult who is willing and able to step in to stop the Bullying, even if doing so is scary or hard.

What Can an Adult Do?

The adults in your life are responsible for protecting you when you can't protect yourself. What can adults do to help you if you're being bullied?

* They can talk to the kid or kids doing the Bullying and insist that they stop.

* They can make the kids doing the Bullying apologize or do something to make up for it.

* They can talk to the parents of the kids doing the Bullying.

* They can talk to the followers of the kid doing the Bullying to convince them not to go along with it.

* They can provide more supervision or remove privileges from the kids doing the Bullying so there's less opportunity for the Bullying to continue.

* They can get other kids involved in making sure that you are protected from Bullying.

* They can offer programs to teach your whole school or community about preventing Bullying.

127

Bullying continues and even gets worse when it's kept a secret. When you break the secrecy, you take away the power of Bullying.

STANDING UP FOR A FRIEND WHO IS BEING BULLIED

What if a friend of yours is being bullied? A lot of kids are afraid to Speak Up in this situation because they don't want to get picked on too. You should only Speak Up directly to a bully if it's safe for you to do so. Here are two examples of how you could stick up for a friend who is being picked on.

If what's happening to your friend is very serious and you don't feel safe confronting the kid doing the Bullying, the best way to help your friend is to tell a caring adult what's going on. Even if your friend says not to tell, you may need to get a grown-up involved to keep your friend safe. Speaking Up to get adult help when needed is an important part of being a good friend.

NOW YOU TRY IT!

Speaking Up by saying what you mean without being mean is a hard skill to master, but it's an important one. It allows your friends to understand you better and helps you get past friendship Rough Spots. Sometimes we need to Speak Up by asking for what we want or by saying no to something we don't want. Speaking Up also means not overreacting to teasing. When a friend teases you in a way you don't like, you can tell your friend how you feel. When someone who is not a friend is teasing you, use one of the responses to teasing to act like you don't care. If you or someone you know is being bullied, meaning the kid doing the Bullying is more powerful than the other kid, then you need to Speak Up to a caring adult.

* Is there a situation where you need to Speak Up, but you haven't so far? What do you think is holding you back from having your say?

* Have you ever yelled at a friend or called your friend names? How did your friend respond? What could you have done instead?

* When you're feeling frustrated, it's tempting to yell. Why is this not a good way to communicate?

* Do you have a habit of apologizing when you didn't do anything wrong? Has anyone said to you, "Stop apologizing!"? A sincere apology is a good way to resolve a conflict, but too much apologizing can be annoying. Can you explain why?

* Why is it sometimes hard to say no to a friend? Have you ever had a situation where you went along with what your friend wanted but later wished you had said no? Which of the *Ways to Say No* would be easiest for you to use with a friend? (Remember, *don't* try these with grown-ups!)

* Have you ever been teased at school? How did you react? Which of the Responses to Teasing would be easiest for you to use?

* Do you know of a Bullying situation where you need to Speak Up to a trusted grown-up to protect yourself or a friend?

PART V
Letting Go to Accept Friends

Letting Go? Oh no! No, sirree! I don't like that idea at all! Once we cats get our claws into something, we do NOT want to Let Go! I want to learn how to make OTHER PEOPLE let go of tasty snacks so I can eat them myself.

I'm pretty sure that's not what this part of the book is about.

Every friendship, no matter how good, will have Friendship Rough Spots. These are times when you and your friends disagree or annoy each other; times when playing together isn't fun; or when your friends just don't want to do what you want them to do. But a Friendship Rough Spot doesn't have to mean the end of a friendship. This part of *Growing Friendships* is about accepting when things don't go your way, or people don't act the way you want them to. It will help you learn ways to get past problems with your friends.

13
Be a Good Sport

SAMIR'S CHALLENGE: ACTING LIKE A SORE LOSER

Samir is so focused on getting on base in the kickball game that he doesn't think about how his arguing affects the others. Accusing someone of cheating never goes over well. Refusing to accept when you're out delays the game and annoys the other players. Samir needs to Let Go of his turn and let someone else be up as kicker.

When the other boy tells him he's out, Samir should just say, "OK," and move on. Even if he thinks he's right, it's not worth ruining the game and irritating everyone else by arguing. Samir doesn't understand that it's better to lose a game than to lose a friend.

Why doesn't Samir accept being out? A lot of kids have trouble handling winning and losing. They brag if they win or they whine and sulk if they lose. They don't understand that winning and losing are temporary—they only last a few seconds—so the important thing is to have fun while playing.

Whether you win or lose, be sure to tell the other players, "Good game!" If you mess up, you should tell yourself, "I can try again the next time we play."

Kids want to play with kids who are able to have fun no matter how the game turns out. Here is another example of poor sportsmanship. Can you figure out what the girl should do instead?

Answer: The first girl should keep playing, cheerfully, even though she's losing. It's hard to handle losing, but wrecking the game and quitting in the middle isn't the right thing to do. When the first girl knocks over the board, it's like she's saying to her friend, "I don't care about the thought and effort you put into this game!" The friend feels annoyed and probably won't want to play checkers with her again. If the first girl had been able to finish the game calmly—even though she was losing—they could have moved on to another fun activity or played checkers again another day.

What should the boy below do differently in this situation?

Answer: The first boy should speak kindly to his friend, especially if the friend is playing badly. The first boy is excited that his character is doing well in this video game, but acting happy when your friend is doing poorly in a game is not kind. Telling someone that they are bad at something is also not a friendly thing to do. This boy should have been sympathetic and encouraging to his friend. He could have said in a kind voice, "Oh! Too bad! You have to start again. Well, keep going! Maybe you'll catch up on the next turn."

Here's one more situation involving being a poor sport. Can you tell how the girl could handle it better?

Answer: The first girl should remember that it's not her job to criticize her friend's playing. She should say nothing or say something kind. It's disappointing when your team loses, but blaming other people is mean—*especially* if it's true that they caused the loss. To be a good sport, this girl should have said something comforting to her teammate like, "It was a nice try!" or "Everyone makes mistakes" or just "Better luck next time!"

KEEP PRACTICING TO LEARN TO HANDLE WINNING AND LOSING

Do you have trouble handling winning and losing games? You may want to try an experiment: When it's a nice day outside, try having a jumping contest with yourself. Draw a starting line on the sidewalk or blacktop and then jump as far as you can and mark the distance. Do this nine more times. What happens? Sometimes you'll beat your own record. Sometimes you won't. But overall, with practice, you'll probably jump farther.

The same thing happens when you play sports or games or compete in any other skilled activity, such as music, art, or even academic subjects. Sometimes you'll win; sometimes you won't. Some days you'll do well; some days you'll mess up. We all have off-days, when we're just not up to our usual level of performance. But if you keep practicing, over time you'll get better.

The key is not to get tangled up by old losses, failures, or disappointments. Doing that will keep you from moving forward. You can't change what has already happened, and continuing to dwell on those bad times will just make you feel discouraged and get in the way of trying again.

LETTING GO OF DISAPPOINTMENT

If you're having trouble *Letting Go* of a time when you didn't do as well as you wanted, try *The Train Trick* to help yourself Let Go of the disappointment. Imagine putting the bad experience on a train. Picture the train picking up speed as it carries the bad experience farther and farther away from you. Imagine the train moving far off into the distance until

137

you can't even see it. The disappointment is over and gone. Then imagine turning your head to look at a new train approaching you. That's your next opportunity to try again.

The Train Trick

14
Respect Others' Choices

NATASHA'S CHALLENGE: TRYING TO CONTROL TOO MUCH

Natasha is acting like an **Enforcer** rather than a friend. She is focusing on what she thinks is right. She thinks she needs to let everyone know her opinion about how things ought to be, but she's not considering what the other kids feel when she bosses them around, scolds them for breaking the rules, or tattles on them. She is acting like she is the boss of the whole school.

Even though Natasha is not yelling or calling anyone names, she is bothering people. Natasha cares about doing the right thing, but her bossiness annoys everyone around her and doesn't help her make or keep friends.

THE ENFORCER EFFECT

The problem with acting like an Enforcer is that most kids have grown-ups—their mom and dad; their grandma and grandpa; their teacher, coach, and babysitter . . . all telling them what to do, so they *really* don't like it when another kid tells them what to do.

If you find yourself saying things like, "It *has* to be this way!" or "You shouldn't do that!" you might be acting like an Enforcer.

Speech bubble (cat): Huh. I kind of like the idea of being an Enforcer. It just works better if everybody does things my way.

Speech bubble (dog): Good luck with that.

WHAT TO DO INSTEAD OF BEING AN ENFORCER

What should Natasha do instead of being an Enforcer? She needs to accept other people's choices, even when she disagrees with them. She needs to Let Go of her wish to control everyone and everything around her. She needs to think about not just "What is right?" but also "What is kind?"

Part of Letting Go of bossiness means remembering to ask questions instead of giving orders.

Ask Questions

Letting Go of bossiness also means reminding yourself that it's not your job to make sure that other kids behave well.

Let the Grown-ups Correct Other Kids

Another very important part of Letting Go of bossiness is being careful to only tell on someone if there's a real danger.

TELLING VERSUS TATTLING

Being a tattletale and trying to get other kids in trouble is not a good way to make friends. You only need to tell a grown-up if

* Someone might get hurt

* Something might get broken

* Someone needs help

* You need help because you've tried to handle a difficult situation on your own, but you haven't been able to solve it.

What if someone is breaking a rule but the teacher doesn't do anything to stop it? That's not your problem. The teacher may have a good reason for not getting involved. If there's no danger, you don't need to say anything. Let It Go.

FIGURE IT OUT

In which of these situations do you think it would be a good idea to tell a grown-up?

a. Bo is chewing gum in school.

b. Alexis cut in front of you in line.

c. Carlin is throwing a ball at the window.

d. Isaac is making annoying noises while you're trying to work. You've asked him two times to stop, but he keeps doing it.

e. Ying fell down on the playground and is crying.

f. Kiersten took the blue marker and you want to use it.

g. Gabriela saved a seat in the cafeteria for her friend, which is against the rules.

h. Some big boys keep tossing around a little boy's lunch box.

Answers: *c*, *e*, and *h* are situations where you need to tell an adult because there's possible danger. *d* is also a situation where you may want to ask for help because you've tried but you haven't been able to handle it on your own.

If a situation doesn't affect you directly, just ignore it. If it *does* affect you but it's not serious, you can either try to handle it on your own with a polite request or Let It Go. Telling an adult should be something you do to get help, not to get someone in trouble.

145

15
Move Past Conflict

JORGE'S CHALLENGE: HOLDING GRUDGES

Jorge is holding a **grudge** against Ethan. A grudge means staying mad at someone for something that happened in the past. Because Ethan was hogging the ball, Jorge has decided he no longer wants to be friends with Ethan. The sad thing is that Ethan probably has no idea what the problem is.

Every friendship has conflict. A conflict happens when two people disagree about something. No two people are ever going to think exactly the same way all the time, so all friends will have disagreements. Also, no one is perfect, so at some point, your friend will probably do something that annoys you and you'll probably do something that annoys your friend.

Whether the friendship continues depends on how you handle conflict. Conflict isn't pleasant, but if you handle it well, it can actually strengthen your friendship by helping you understand each other better.

Jorge pulled out of the friendship without giving Ethan a chance to make things better. Non-friends don't necessarily care, but friends usually want to work things out if you have a *Friendship Rough Spot*. Here are some kind ways Jorge could have handled the conflict to keep Ethan as his friend:

KIND WAYS TO HANDLE CONFLICT

Give your friend another chance.

Ask for what you want.

Accept the way your friend is.

Do something different together.

Notice that some of these are **"*inside*" *strategies*,** which are focused on how Jorge thinks about the situation, and some are **"*outside*" *strategies*,** which involve talking directly to Ethan.

You don't always have to act on a problem. Sometimes the best solution is to change how you view it. If you decide to talk to your friend about a problem—maybe because it happens often or because it bothers you a lot—be sure to express your concerns in a way that's easy for your friend to accept.

HOW NOT TO TALK TO A FRIEND ABOUT A PROBLEM

Here are some ways *not* to talk about a problem with a friend. In these examples, the kids are doing things that make their problems worse.

Can you explain why? How will their friends react? What should they do instead?

YELLING AND CALLING NAMES

When we feel angry, it's tempting to turn up the volume. This girl is shouting insults at her friend. Her friend is not going to want to listen to what she's saying and she'll probably yell back. Having a shouting match definitely won't solve their problem. That's just loud noise, and it could make the problem even worse. Also, calling someone names is mean. It's hurtful and never helpful.

BRINGING UP MANY AND LONG-PAST ISSUES

This boy waited weeks to say anything about a problem. His friend probably doesn't even remember what happened and will feel like these accusations are an attack that came out of nowhere. If you decide to bring up an issue with a friend, you need to do it right when it happens or within a day or two.

Also, it's best to bring up only one issue at a time. Sometimes kids think that if they build up their courage to bring up one problem, they should mention all of them. This won't work because it feels overwhelming to the listener. No one wants to hear, "Here's what you did wrong. Here's another thing you did wrong. And another. And another . . ." That feels like an avalanche of criticism rather than an effort to work things out.

COMPLAINING ABOUT A FRIEND TO OTHERS

This girl is talking about her friend behind her back. That's not kind. And it won't help because the problem can only be solved by this girl and the friend she's upset with—they're the ones who are directly involved in the problem. This girl should choose a time when no one else is around to talk things over with that friend. If she mentions the problem in front of other kids, her friend will feel embarrassed and angry. No one likes to be criticized in front of an audience.

Talking over a problem with a friend is not about blasting her with anger, getting even, or convincing her that she's a jerk. To solve a problem, you need to talk directly but gently to your friend about one issue when you can be private. Doing this means you need to Let Go of the idea that your friend should already know what's wrong. It also means Letting Go of your anger so you can speak calmly and kindly to your friend.

What should you say?

Telling people you don't like something they're doing is a criticism. It's hard to hear a criticism. When people feel criticized, they usually respond with excuses like, "It's not my fault!" "He made me do it!" or "You did something worse!"

THE RIGHT WAY TO DISCUSS A PROBLEM WITH A FRIEND

If you want your friend to hear your concern, you should express your criticism in a way that gets around the need to make excuses. Here's a formula for a *Soft Criticism*:

1. Give an Excuse
By giving your friend an excuse before you mention the bad behavior, you're taking away the friend's need to come up with excuses. You're also telling the friend, "I know you're a good person, even when you mess up!" Here are some possible excuses you could use:

"I'm sure you didn't mean to . . ."

"You probably didn't realize . . ."

"I know you were trying to . . ."

"I understand that it's hard for you to . . ."

2. Explain the Problem
Now comes the part where you describe what your friend did that you didn't like and how it affected you.

"But when you [friend's bad behavior], I . . ."

3. Ask for What You Want
There's no point dwelling on the past. What matters is what happens next. Here are some ways to ask for what you want going forward.

"Could you please . . . ?"

"Next time can we . . . ?"

Here's an example of a girl doing a Soft Criticism.

Give an Excuse

Explain the Problem

Ask for What You Want

How would you finish the sentence in the cartoon above? What should she ask her friend to do from now on? How about, ". . . keep it private if I tell you something embarrassing?"

Now try this one:

Give an Excuse

Explain the Problem

Ask for What You Want

How would you finish the sentence in the cartoon above? What should the boy ask his friend to do from now on? How about, ". . . leave my food alone?"

APOLOGIZING FOR YOUR PART IN THE CONFLICT

Discussing the problem, starting with a Soft Criticism, is one good way to handle conflict. Another way is to apologize. When friends have a conflict, there are always two sides to the story. Maybe your friend did or said something less than kind, but chances are that you did too. The person who is *least* wrong should apologize first because it's easier for that person. A sincere apology is a good way to get past a Friendship Rough Spot.

An apology only works if you mean it. Can you figure out what's wrong with these apologies?

Just saying sorry doesn't seem sincere, especially if you yell it or mutter it. Be sure to tell your friend exactly what you're sorry for doing. Try not to use the word "but" because that takes away from your apology. "I'm sorry, but . . ." sounds like you're not really sorry. And definitely don't blame your friend for what *you* did wrong.

If you can, offer to do something to make up for your mistake or promise to do something different from now on. The kids in this cartoon do a better job apologizing.

When you apologize to a friend, your friend will usually apologize to you too. But even if your friend doesn't apologize, you'll know that you did the right thing to try to mend the friendship.

When my owner scolds me for eating something I shouldn't, I put my tail between legs and whimper an apology.

Good point.

Cats aren't good at apologies. When my owner scolds me for scratching the furniture, I just stare at her and flick my tail. Why do humans have so much furniture anyway, if they don't want cats to scratch it?

THE POWER OF FORGIVENESS

So far we've focused on handling conflict by talking things out. But sometimes the kindest thing to do is to just forgive your friend. If you keep a mental list of every bad thing your friend has ever done, you are hurting yourself by carrying bitterness in your heart. **Forgiveness** helps your friend, but it also helps you by freeing you to think about more interesting and more important things.

Forgiveness is a generous thing to do. It doesn't mean pretending that the bad event didn't happen. It just means accepting that everyone makes mistakes and treating the friend the way you like to be treated. It means Letting Go of anger because you care about a friend.

Part of being a good friend is not holding on to grudges. Here are some guidelines about when to forgive someone.

Forgiveness Guidelines

*   If it only happened one time, and it probably won't happen again, Let It Go.

*   If your friend didn't do it on purpose, Let It Go.

*   If it wasn't that bad, Let It Go.

*   If your friend is really sorry, Let It Go.

*   If it was just a mistake, and the friend is usually kind, Let It Go.

*   If it happened more than a month ago, definitely Let It Go.

Most conflicts between kids are solved by letting some time pass for tempers to cool and then trying again. If you decide to forgive your friend, you don't have to make a big announcement about it. The next time you see your friend, just act friendly, smile, do something fun together, or invite your friend over.

WHEN FRIENDSHIPS END

Sometimes friendships end despite your best efforts. It happens to almost everyone. Some friendships end with a big argument; some friendships just fade away. When friends are in different classes, when their interests change in different directions, or when they just don't spend much time together anymore, they tend to drift apart.

The most painful end to a friendship is when one person decides not to be friends and the other still wants to be friends. Unfortunately, you can't force someone to be your friend. If someone rejects you again and again, you may have to Let Go of the idea of being friends with that person.

The end of a friendship is often sad, but it's not always a bad thing. Friends who have a lot of arguments or who tend to get each other in trouble may be better off separating. When being with someone is more painful than fun, it's a sign that you might need to find a different friend.

It's understandable if you're feeling upset because a friendship has ended. It's hard to lose a friend. If you were good friends before, you might become good friends again some day. But the important thing is, you don't have to stay lonely.

Sometimes Letting Go of one friendship makes room for other friendships to grow. Have you ever tried something new and decided you liked it—maybe a new activity or a new ice cream flavor? If you hadn't been brave enough to try it, you might never have discovered how much you like it. You may find the same thing with a new friend.

Whether it's with an old friend or a new friend, friendship is worth finding and keeping. That means that we need to Let Go of anger, sadness, and fear and hold on to the real caring that's at the heart of friendship.

NOW YOU TRY IT!

Letting Go means being flexible enough to accept when things don't go exactly how you want them to go. It also means being kind enough not to point out people's mistakes in public or in a way that hurts them. We talked about Letting Go of poor sportsmanship, Letting Go of bossiness, and Letting Go of grudges. Letting Go means not staying mad. It also means accepting your friends the way they are, rather than how you think they ought to be. That's a kind thing to do!

* Why is it a good idea to avoid correcting someone in front of others?

* Can you think of a time when you really believed you were right and your friend was wrong? How did you—or could you—get past this disagreement?

* Have you ever held on to a grudge about something that the other person has probably forgotten? How did holding on to this grudge affect you? How did it affect the other person?

* Have you ever done something that upset a friend? How did you feel afterward? Did your friend forgive you?

* Have you ever had a friendship end? What happened?

* How can you tell when you should Let Go of your anger and forgive a friend versus when you need to Let Go of a friendship and find different friends?

167

Final Thoughts

Good friends make happy times more fun and hard times more bearable. But friendships aren't always easy. Luckily, you've learned a lot from this book, so you're ready to handle those Friendship Rough Spots. We'll leave you with three final pieces of advice:

1. Be open to friendship.

There are many different kinds of friendships: friends you play with, friends you laugh with, friends you work with, friends you talk with . . . Each of these friendships makes your life more fun and more meaningful. But you'll only find new friendships if you're open to getting to know other people and letting them get to know you.

2. Choose good friends.

Pay attention to how you feel about yourself when you're with your friends. Good friends make you feel like you matter to them. They aren't perfect—they may sometimes do or say things that upset you—but they care about what you think and how you feel. If the friends you have now aren't good friends because they often make you feel bad, keep looking! Good friends are out there.

3. Be a good friend.

To have good friends, you need to be a good friend. This means thinking about what your friends want as well as what you want, and always trying to make the kind choice. Kindness is the key to friendship.

ACKNOWLEDGMENTS

This book was a delight to write! We laughed so much that we were often afraid we might get kicked out of the Bucks County Free Library in Yardley, Pennsylvania! But beyond the fun, what drove us to write this book is our deep commitment to helping children make and keep friends. Friends make the hard times more bearable and the good times more fun. They help us become our best selves and give meaning and richness to our lives. When we teach children to build deep and satisfying friendships, we give them the tools they need to create their own happiness.

The contents of this book draw as much as possible from research on children's friendships as well as Eileen's work with clients in her private practice as a clinical psychologist in Princeton, New Jersey.

We'd like to thank our wonderful agents, Stefanie von Borstel and Taylor Martindale Kean of Full Circle Literary, for believing in this book and enthusiastically working to get it out in the world. We'd also like to thank our insightful editors, Nicole Geiger, Lindsay Brown, and Jade Chan, for their wise advice on the manuscript, and our illustrator, Cathi Mingus, for bringing our characters to life.

We'd also like to thank all the children and parents we've known who have generously spoken with us about their friendship concerns so we could make this book real and relevant. Most of all, we'd like to thank our families: Chris's husband, Bill, and their sons, Joey, Tommy, and Will; and Eileen's husband, Tony, and their children, Mary, Daniel, Sheila, and Brenna. Our families' love, support, and inspiration is invaluable to us.

Eileen Kennedy-Moore, PhD, and Christine McLaughlin

ADDITIONAL RESOURCES FROM DR. KENNEDY-MOORE

FOR KIDS

What About Me?: 12 Ways To Get Your Parents' Attention (Without Hitting Your Sister) by Eileen Kennedy-Moore and Mits Katayama (Parenting Press, 2005)

Online questions and answers about friendship for kids: www.DrFriendtastic.com

FOR PARENTS

Raising Emotionally and Socially Healthy Kids by Eileen Kennedy-Moore (Great Courses, Teaching Company, DVD, 2014). Also available as a CD or video/audio download at thegreatcourses.com /courses/raising-emotionally-and-socially-healthy -kids.html.

Smart Parenting for Smart Kids: Nurturing Your Child's True Potential by Eileen Kennedy-Moore and Mark S. Lowenthal (Jossey-Bass/Wiley, 2011)

The Unwritten Rules of Friendship: Simple Strategies to Help Your Child Make Friends by Natalie Madorsky Elman and Eileen Kennedy-Moore (Little, Brown, 2003)

Growing Friendships blog on Psychology Today website: www.Growing FriendshipsBlog.com

Growing Friendships monthly email newsletter for parents, teachers, and counselors: tinyurl.com/EKM-news

GLOSSARY

apology: Saying you're sorry when you've done something to hurt or upset a friend. A sincere apology is a good way to get past a Friendship Rough Spot.

Believe the Best: Believing that your friend probably wasn't trying to hurt you when they did something you didn't like. Believing the Best is a kind and generous way to look at friends, and it helps you be less angry.

Blending In: One of the five main friendship skills. It involves knowing how to join a group activity or conversation, get along with partners or teammates, and contribute to group fun.

Bullying: Deliberate meanness aimed at a specific person, often repeated over time, *and* involving a Power Difference between the kid doing the mean acts and the target of those acts.

Common Ground: The things you and another kid both like. This is where friendships grow.

Compromise: Doing partly what you want and partly what your friend wants.

conflict: When two people disagree about something. Conflict isn't pleasant, but if you handle it well, it can actually strengthen your friendship by helping you understand each other better.

Emergency Calming Strategies: Strategies that will quickly take your mind off whatever is upsetting you. These can help you avoid crying in public and calm down so you can think clearly. They include breathing, distraction, and taking a break.

Enforcer: Someone who bosses others around, scolds them for breaking the rules, or tattles on them.

Filter: An object that lets some things pass through and holds other things back. We want our own internal Filter to work as much as it can so that only kind words come through our lips.

forgiveness: Letting Go of anger after someone has hurt or upset us. It doesn't mean pretending that the bad behavior didn't happen. It just means accepting that everyone makes mistakes and being willing to move on.

Friendship Rough Spot: When friends disagree, upset, or annoy each other. Rough Spots happen in all friendships, but they don't have to mean the end of a relationship.

grudge: When you stay mad at someone for something they did or said from the past. Holding onto your angry or hurt feelings.

honest compliment: Telling someone that you like or admire something about him or her. Compliments don't have to be long or complicated, but they must be honest. If someone gives you a compliment, be sure to smile and say, "Thanks!"

"inside" strategies: Coping strategies that involve thinking about a difficult situation in a way that makes you less upset.

interested questions: Questions that show you want to know more about someone. The best questions to ask begin with *what* or *how*.

"I" Statements: Comments that begin with the word "I" and describe what you think, feel, or want, without criticizing anyone else.

Letting Go: One of the five main friendship skills. It involves being able to accept when things don't go your way or people don't do what you want them to do. Examples include being a good sport about losing, not correcting others, moving past conflict by forgiving friends.

Magnet Myth of Friendship: The false belief that in order to get friends you have to be so amazing and wonderful that friends are drawn to you the way a magnet attracts metal. The Magnet Myth doesn't work because friendship is about enjoying each other's company rather than proving how great you are.

Match the Tone: Joining a conversation by picking up on the feeling of the conversation and saying something that has a similar feeling.

The Maybe Game: Playing The Maybe Game involves thinking of possible explanations for other kids' behavior other than, "They were trying to be mean!" This can help you avoid getting mad. Most of the time when other kids do something that you don't like, it's an accident or a misunderstanding, or they just didn't realize it would upset you.

Non-friends: Kids who don't know each other well and don't particularly like each other.

Nonsense Word Insults: Nonsense Word Insults are silly and pointless phrases. They are useful when you are trying to practice responding to teasing. They don't mean anything, so if your practice partner says them to you, you won't feel upset, which makes it easier to practice responding calmly to teasing.

Octopus Friend: A very demanding, controlling friend who makes the other person feel trapped. Octopus Friends are afraid of losing their friend so they try to hold on tightly. This often ends up making their friend want to escape.

"outside" strategies: Coping strategies that involve talking or doing something to handle a difficult situation.

Power Difference: When one kid is bigger, older, stronger, tougher, or more popular than another kid. A Power Difference is what makes it hard for kids who are bullied to defend or protect themselves.

Reaching Out: One of the five main friendship skills. It involves trying to connect with other kids to make new friends by greeting them, asking interested questions, giving compliments, and doing small kindnesses, while being careful not to overwhelm them by doing too much too soon.

small kindness: Small actions that show people you like them and want to be friends. These include sharing or helping.

social mistakes: Trying to be friendly but doing something that others find annoying or boring. Examples include making an irritating noise, telling a joke that people don't think is funny, or going on and on about something that others don't find interesting. Everyone makes social mistakes sometimes. That's OK as long as we stop when we see that others aren't enjoying what we're saying or doing.

Soft Criticism: A gentle way to discuss a problem with a friend. The steps are: 1) Give an excuse, 2) Explain the problem, and 3) Ask for what you want.

Speaking Up: One of the five main friendship skills. It involves being able to say what you mean without being mean. Examples include being able to ask for what you want, say no when you need to, and handle teasing and Bullying.

Stepping Back: One of the five main friendship skills. It involves knowing how to stop—and when you need to stop—so you can keep the friends you make. Examples of Stepping Back include being able to stop doing annoying behavior, handle conflict without yelling, and avoid crying in public.

Stop Signals: When someone lets you know that they want you to stop doing whatever you are doing. Stop signals may involve words, such as a polite request or an angry demand. They may also involve the face or body, such as frowning or turning away. If you ignore Stop Signals, other people might get very mad at you.

The Train Trick: A strategy to help you Let Go of a disappointment. Imagine putting the bad experience on a train that carries the bad experience farther and farther away from you.

Watch Then Blend: The secret to joining a group. Stand nearby and watch what the kids are doing, and then slide into the action without interrupting it.

Yes-No Argument: An argument where the words just go back and forth between two or more people, but no one is listening and nothing is getting solved.

ABOUT THE AUTHORS

Eileen Kennedy-Moore, PhD, is an author, psychologist, and mom of four. She is a trusted expert on parenting and child development who is frequently featured in major media, such as the *New York Times*, the *Washington Post*, and *Live with Kelly and Ryan*. Her most recent books for children are *Moody Moody Cars* and *Growing Feelings: A Kids' Guide to Dealing with Emotions about Friends and Other Kids* (written with Christine McLaughlin). She has also written four books for parents. Her books have been translated into ten languages. Dr. Kennedy-Moore is the creator of the *Kids Ask Dr. Friendtastic* podcast, which features friendship advice for kids. Her blog, *Growing Friendships*, on Psychology Today, has over 4.9 million views. Dr. Kennedy-Moore has a private practice in Princeton, New Jersey (lic. #35SI00425400), where she works with adults, children, and families.

Check out EileenKennedyMoore.com.

Christine McLaughlin is a mom to three boys, as well as a prolific writer, editor, and author. With several hundred nonfiction articles to her credit—published in popular magazines and websites—her written work focuses mainly on parenting and health topics. She is the author of eight books including *Growing Feelings: A Kids' Guide to Dealing with Emotions about Friends and Other Kids* (written with Dr. Eileen Kennedy-Moore), *The Dog Lover's Companion to Philadelphia*, and *American Red Cross: Dog First Aid* and *American Red Cross: Cat First Aid*. She and her family live in the Philadelphia area.

Check out ChristineMcLaughlin.net.

GROWING FEELINGS

A KIDS' GUIDE TO
Dealing with Emotions about Friends and Other Kids

By Dr. Eileen Kennedy-Moore
& Christine McLaughlin

A CLEAR, USEFUL, AND ENTERTAINING
TOOLKIT FOR CHILDREN ABOUT
UNDERSTANDING THEIR OWN AND
OTHERS' FEELINGS SO THEY CAN
BUILD MEANINGFUL AND JOYFUL
RELATIONSHIPS. FILLED WITH
CARTOONS AND RESEARCH-BASED TIPS.

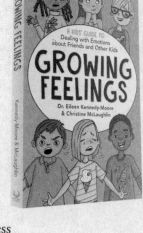

* Feeling Anxious about Friends
* The Opposites of Anxiety Are
  Excitement, Curiosity, and Playfulness
* Feeling Angry about Friends
* The Opposites of Anger Are Acceptance,
  Compassion, and Bigger-Than-Me Happiness
* Feeling Sad about Friends
* The Opposites of Sadness Are Contentment,
  Gratitude, and Hope

"A clear and compassionate
guide that will help kids understand
their emotions and the role they
play in building and maintaining
friendships."

Lisa Damour, PhD, author of *Untangled,*
Under Pressure, and *The Emotional*
Lives of Teenagers